CORNWALL FOR FREE

Over 100 ways of making the most of Cornwall that cost absolutely nothing

Rachael Rowe

CONTENTS

INTRODUCTION

Cornwall is one of the best places in Britain to spend a holiday or weekend break. Costs often add up with catering and admission charges to some attractions. This small book has a wealth of places to go that are free, assuming that visitors have already budgeted for transport and accommodation. In some places the car parks have charges; however it is often possible to park safely along a road without causing an obstruction. Other places are along good walking routes.

Using this book, visitors to Cornwall can discover some of the hidden natural beauty the county has to offer and the history and heritage that makes Cornwall so special. A holiday in Cornwall on a budget opens up a world of opportunity and sometimes different perspectives on the county. As the old saying goes- the best things in life are free. Money saved on a free activity can also make paying attractions more affordable and so for some visitors mixing both free and chargeable activities makes sense for a holiday budget.

Safety advice for the coast and countryside is there for a reason so take note of tides, lifeguard flags and warnings, and the notices about dangerous cliffs. Don't forget to heed the Countryside Code and to respect other people's property.

There are many events and displays in Cornwall that are free but accept donations for charity and a small offering is always appreciated. As with most things the pricing structure in some places is reviewed on a regular basis and whilst the content of the book was checked prior to publication price charges can and do change from time to time. It is advisable to check opening times before travelling as they are variable and subject to change.

Above all, enjoy yourself as you discover Cornwall for free.

ABOUT THE AUTHOR

Rachael Rowe was born and brought up in Cornwall and lives in the South West of England.

DISCLAIMER

Although the author has taken all reasonable care in preparing this book we make no warranty about the accuracy or completeness of its content and, to the maximum extent permitted, disclaim all liability arising from its use.

If you do find that a pricing structure has changed or perhaps you have discovered a new free attraction in Cornwall please email cornwallforfree@mail.com so that the e-book can be updated.

TEN OF CORNWALL'S BEST KEPT FREE SECRETS

- **Take A Walk or Cycle Ride along The Camel Way**

  Covering 18 miles of some of Cornwall's lesser known beauty spots this walking and cycling trail alongside the disused Camel Valley railway line is a real find and a wonderful way to spend a day in the Cornish countryside. The trail is also suitable for disabled access and is an excellent place to spot birds. Visitors can walk the whole eighteen miles from Bodmin or do a shorter five mile route from Wadebridge to Padstow.

- **Explore Art Galleries in St Ives**

  Artists came to St Ives in the early part of the twentieth century, attracted by the extraordinary light. Walk around the narrow streets and wander into the many galleries that are dotted all over town with up and coming as well as established artists at work in the studios. Many have free admission and are very welcoming.

- **See the Merry Maidens**

  Legend has it that a group of dancing girls were turned to stone for dancing on the Sabbath and today the nineteen granite stones are in a rare perfect circle near St Buryan on the B3315 Newlyn to Lands' End road where they have stood for centuries. In a field to the north east of the Maidens are two further standing stones, said to be the pipers who played music whilst the maids danced, and a further stone known as the Blind Fiddler to the west. The origin of these ancient standing stones are uncertain but are thought to date from Bronze Age times and the legend invented by the early Christian Church to help prevent pagan behaviour.

- **Visit Truro Cathedral**

  Towering above the rooftops of Truro the cathedral dominates the skyline and is very interesting to visit. Visitors can join a service or visit in the gaps when a service is not being held. Admission is free to the cathedral with a voluntary donation system.

  Opening times: Mon-Sat 07.30-18.00, Sun 9.00-19.00. Check the website for services

  www.trurocathedral.org.uk

- **Catch Crabs**

  Seaside towns and many beaches are wonderful for fishing in rock pools and off harbour walls for crabs and shrimps. Armed with a bucket and crab line this can provide hours of free fun for a family.

- **Listen to a Male Voice Choir on the Harbour at Polperro**

  Polperro is just one seaside town that has a tradition of the local choir singing on the harbour side in summer. In Polperro this occurs most Wednesday evenings and is a delight to hear as the sun goes down over the sea.

- **See the Christmas Lights at Mousehole**

  Each December the harbour at Mousehole is festooned with decorative lights that attract visitors for miles around. Boats and the village itself are illuminated in a spectacular display, apart from the evening of December 22nd when the lights are dimmed for an hour as Mousehole remembers the crew of the Penlee Lifeboat who were tragically killed attempting to rescue others in December 1981. www.mouseholelights.org.uk

- **Learn About Local History in Perranzabuloe**

  Beyond the surf scene in Perranporth lies the small but fascinating Perranzabuloe Museum. Visitors can find out the history of the area, see a traditional Cornish kitchen and learn about the important role the area had during the Second World War, as well as some of the famous personalities associated with this area. www.perranzabuloemuseum.co.uk

- **Have a Picnic at Marazion Beach**

  Set against the stunning backdrop of St Michaels Mount the beach at Marazion is a beautiful place to spend a sunny day and enjoy a picnic on the sand. Have a swim in the sea and if the tide is out walk across the causeway to St Michaels Mount. Watch out for the tides so that you can return by foot. Alternatively the shuttle boat is available at a charge.

- **Explore the Gardens at Mount Edgcombe**

  Whilst there is a charge to visit the house at Mount Edgcombe the magnificent gardens beside the River

Tamar are free and a spectacular place to spend an afternoon. The free area includes most of the formal gardens and also the National Camellia Collection, making spring a wonderful time to visit.

GREAT ATTRACTIONS

There are lots of places all over Cornwall that have free admission to visitors. These are just a small selection.

CORNISH GOLDSMITHS TREASURE PARK

Address: Tolgus Mill, near Redruth, Cornwall, TR16 4HN

Phone: 01209 203280

Website: www.treasureparks.com

Opening times: Mon-Sat 9.30-17.30, Sun 10.00-16.00

Built on the site of the Tolgus Tin Mine and in a picturesque setting Treasure Parks has a number of interesting things to do for all the family. There are jewellery displays and visitors can also pan for gold here and take a 4D haunted mine ride. The old mine workings and history are another interesting aspect to the complex as are the one off displays. With restaurants and shops here too it is a good place to escape from the rain.

ST CATHERINE'S CASTLE, FOWEY

Phone: 0117 9750 700 (Regional office)

Website: www.english-heritage.org.uk

Opening times: During daylight hours

Probably one of the smallest forts in England, St Catherine's Castle was built by Henry VIII in the 1530's. Two guns were added in the Crimean War and it was further developed in

World War Two. It is an interesting place to visit with some lovely views across the river.

HEARTLANDS PROJECT

Address: Heartlands, Robinson's Shaft, Dudnance Lane, Pool, Cornwall, TR15 3QY

Phone: 01209 722322

Website: www.heartlandscornwall.com

Opening times: April to September 10.00-17.00 every day. October to March 10.00-16.00 every day. Check the website for details of evening events throughout the year.

The newly developed Heartlands Project at Pool has some fascinating displays of mining as it was traditionally done before the tin and copper mines closed in this part of West Cornwall. There are also tours of an engine house and many more interesting things to see and do. With a social history soundscape and geological exhibits, not to mention displays of mining equipment this is a very interesting place to learn about the industrial history of Cornwall. Although the attraction is free there is a charge for parking and so finding a place on a nearby street is an option.

PLACES TO ENJOY THE SUNSET

ZENNOR

Why not drive or walk into the sunset by taking the B3390 road from St Ives to Zennor. On a clear evening the Atlantic Ocean stretches out in front of you and the sun setting on the water will throw up a spectrum of colours. The next stop out to sea is America. The road is narrow and the farmland stretches over the cliff tops making it a very romantic place to ask an important question.

HELMAN TOR

Located near Bodmin

Grid ref: SX062615

This area forms part of the Helman Tor Nature Reserve and is full of birds and plant species. Climbing to the Tor summit gives sweeping views across Bodmin Moor to include the Brown Willy, Rough Tor and even the South Coast on a good day. Watching the sun set over the moorland is a delight.

GOONHILLY DOWNS, LIZARD PENINSULA

The Lizard Peninsula is a spectacularly beautiful place to explore. The Goonhilly Earth Station has distinctive satellite dishes on Goonhilly Downs that dominate the landscape. Driving on the B3293 from Helston at twilight is a surreal experience. The dishes often give the appearance of a scene from War of the Worlds and set against a dramatic sunset this is a sight worth taking time to experience.

ANCIENT CORNWALL

Cornwall's ancient past is steeped in history from the Druids and Celts and there are places of significant interest all over the county that can be visited for free. There are relics from the Bronze Age and many full of legend as to how they got there in the first place.

ROCHE ROCK CHAPEL

The site around Roche Rock appears to have had religious significance for centuries and there has been activity here since prehistoric times. Roche Rock Chapel stands on a rocky outcrop overlooking the village of Roche and was built in the fifteenth century. It is dedicated to St Michael and the reasons as to why it was placed there are unknown. The ruined Roche Rock Chapel can be reached by public footpath from Roche village.

THE HURLERS

Grid Ref: SX 258 174

Close to the village of Minions stand three large stone circles. These are believed to be groups of people turned to stone for playing the game of hurling on the Sabbath and close to them is a pair of standing stones which are thought to be pipers. The stones date from the early Bronze Age and are in alignment to several of the nearby tors.

MEN AN TOL

Address: Madron, Cornwall

Grid Ref: SW 4265 3494

The Men an Tol or stone with a hole is on moorland near Madron in West Cornwall. Its origins are unclear but it is thought to date from the Bronze Age and may have been used in ancient rituals or be part of a stone circle, perhaps providing a link to a sacred hill nearby. Holed stones are relatively rare in Cornwall. It is rumoured to be able to cure a number of ailments including rickets and back pain.

THE CHEESWRING

Grid Ref: SX 258723

Around four miles north of Liskeard on the eastern edge of Bodmin Moor stands the Cheesewring, a granite tor formed naturally by weathering. Legend has it that it is the result of a battle between a giant and a man, and the stones are so called because they resemble the rocks used in cheese making. A walk combining both this site and the Hurlers is a great way of exploring the Minions area.

LANYON QUOIT

Grid Ref: SW 430 337

Located on the Madron to Morvah Road west of Penzance the ancient dolmen of Lanyon Quoit is a remarkable sight and dates from the Neolithic period (3500-2500BC).

CASTLE AN DINAS

Address: St Columb Major, Cornwall

Grid Reference: SW 9455 6237

Castle an Dinas is an ancient Iron Age hill fort located on Castle Downs and with magnificent views of the Cornish landscape. Legend has it that this was once the seat of the ancient King of Cornwall, and that King Arthur's mother Ygraine was killed here along with Cador, Duke of Cornwall. This is an impressive site to walk around with its ramparts, ditches and Bronze Age barrows. Castle An Dinas is accessible via two footpaths from both southern and northerly directions.

CHUN CASTLE

Address: Morvah, Cornwall

Grid Reference: SW 4050 3395

Another impressive Iron Age fort, Chun Castle has magnificent views of the Atlantic and Mounts Bay from its location on Chun Downs. Excavations in the area indicate the site was occupied during the 2nd and 3rd centuries and there is also evidence of Roman occupation. The site was one of the main defences of West Cornwall and is accessed from open heathland and by several footpaths in the area.

HALLIGGYE FOGOU

Address: Trelowarren Estate, Mawgan, TR12 6AF

Opening times: Daylight hours from April to September. Closed from October to March. Bring a torch.

Halliggye Fogou is one of the best preserved and most interesting underground networks in Cornwall. It is believed to have originated during the Iron Age and may have been used to store things or in rituals. The Fogou is located in the Trelowarren Estate and is 5 miles south east of Helston on the B3293. Trelowarren is accessible by bus and bicycle.

TREGESEAL STONE CIRCLE

Address: St Just, Cornwall

Grid Reference: SW 3863 3237

Standing on the slopes of Truthwall Common outside St Just is the Tregeseal Stone Circle. Just to the south of Carn Kenidjack, they are believed to be part of a ritualistic formation. The alternative names for the stone circle are Nine Maidens and the Dancing Stones. There is an ancient Bronze Age barrow nearby and these stones are thought to have originated from that time or from the late Neolithic period.

CRAFT WORKSHOPS AND ART GALLERIES

Cornwall has inspired artists for years and the Newlyn and St Ives Schools are renowned the world over. Many of the workshops and galleries are open to the public and in some there are often demonstrations of the crafts.

SERPENTINE WORKSHOPS, THE LIZARD

A visit to the beaches around The Lizard will reveal the distinctive serpentine stone which is a unique metamorphic green rock with red and white veins thrown up from beneath the earth's crust. The stone has been fashioned into ornaments, paperweights and other decorative items by craft workers. There are a few workshops left in the Lizard area now where serpentine working or turning can be seen and this old craft appreciated.

ART GALLERIES, ST JUST

Website: www.just-art.co.uk

St Just in Penwith has a thriving community of artists in this beautiful town just a few miles from Lands' End. From pottery to paintings, jewellery and fabrics there are several interestng workshops to explore in the St Just area and see how the surrounding countryside has inspired the art that is being produced.

FALMOUTH ART GALLERY

Address: Falmouth Art Gallery, Municipal Building, The Moor, Falmouth, TR11 4SN

Phone: 01326 313863

Website: www.falmouthartgallery.com

Opening times: Mon-Sat 10.00-17.00 including public holidays

One of the most important collections of art in Cornwall this museum has work by Charles Napier, Sir Edward Coley Burne Jones, Dame Laura Knight, Henry Scott Tuke, Sir Alfred Munnings, and more. There are seasonal exhibits as well as the permanent collection and a shop.

PENLEE HOUSE GALLERY AND MUSEUM

Address: Penlee House Gallery and Museum, Morrab Road, Penzance, TR18 4HE

Phone: 01736 363625

Website: www.penleehouse.org.uk

Opening Times: Monday to Saturday 10.00-17.00. Admission is free on Saturday only.

Penlee House is free on Saturdays only and is an excellent place to see the Newlyn School of Art at its finest. Artists inspired by the area include Lamorna Birch, Alfred Munnings and Walter Langley, and are amongst the many painters with work on display. There are photographic exhibits too including Frith, and also local archaeology and other artefacts. Penlee House has good access for wheelchairs.

COWHOUSE GALLERY, PERRANUTHNOE

Address: Lynfield Craft Centre, Perranuthnoe, Cornwall, TR20 9NE

Phone: 01736 710538

Website: www.cowhousegallery.org.uk

Opening times: October to March 10.00-16.00, Otherwise 10.00-17.00

Located in the beautiful village of Perranuthnoe the Cowhouse Gallery is run by local artists and craftspeople. It is full of inspirational pieces of art and a delight to view. The nearby beach of Perranuthnoe is a lovely place for a walk whilst in the area and just a bit further along the coast Prussia Cove is another beautiful place to explore.

NEWLYN ART GALLERY

Address: New Road, Newlyn, TR18 5PZ

Phone: 01736 363715

Website: www.newlynartgallery.co.uk

Opening times: Mon-Sat 10.00-17.00

Located in Newlyn this gallery is regularly home to some interesting art exhibitions.

THE EXCHANGE

Address: Princes Street, Penzance

Phone: 01736 363715

Website: www.newlynartgallery.co.uk

Opening times: Mon-Sat 10.00-17.00

This modern gallery in Penzance is linked to the Newlyn Arts Gallery and has exhibitions throughout the year.

MELINSEY MILL

Address: Melinsey Mill, Veryan, near Truro, TR2 5PX

Phone: 01872 501049

Website: www.melinseymill.co.uk

Opening times: April to October 10.00-17.30

There has been a mill on site since 1210 and Melinsey Mill is a wonderful place to visit in Cornwall. This is a working and restored sixteenth century watermill and also has arts and crafts on display including willow work. The mill is free to visit and the tea and cakes are an additional treat to purchase, ideally after a walk in the area. Do check the website for pizza evenings.

CORNWALL CRAFTS ASSOCIATION AT TRELOWARREN

Address: Trelowarren Estate, Mawgan, Helston, TR12 6AF

Phone: 01326 221224

Website: www.trelowarren.com

Trelowarren is a beautiful country estate which has housed the main exhibition areas for Cornwall Crafts Association. Visitors can view the art on display and also walk in the grounds along many of the woodland trails. Trelowarren also has an excellent restaurant which is the perfect treat after a walk in the woods.

INTERESTING MUSEUMS

BODMIN TOWN MUSEUM

Address: Bodmin Town Museum, Mount Folly, PL31 2HQ,

Phone: 01208 77067

Opening times: From Easter to the end of September; Mon-Fri 10.30 – 16-30, Saturday 10.30-14.30. October- March; Mon-Sat 10.30-14.30. Closed on Sundays and public holidays

This is a fascinating local history museum which features a Cornish kitchen, Victoriana, local rocks and minerals, items from the fire service, reminders of World War Two and many more. Admission is free.

CONSTANTINE HERITAGE COLLECTION

Address: The Tolmen Centre, Fore Street, Constantine TR11 5AA.

Phone: 01326 340279

Opening times: Monday- Thursday 10.30 – 15.30. Closed from Christmas to New Year

For a fascinating historical collection the community museum in Constantine near Helston is worth visiting. Memories from cricket to bowling, bands, quarrying, farming and religion are displayed here. Admission is free and there is a small bookshop.

HELSTON FOLK MUSEUM

Address: Helston Folk Museum, Old Butter Market, Market Place, Helston, TR13 8TH

Phone: 01326 564027

Opening times: All year; Mon-Sat 10.00- 13.00. Closed for a week at Christmas.

Holiday periods;Easter, Summer, Autumn half term, first three weeks in December

Mon, Tues, Thur, Fri 10.00-16.00. Wed, Sat 10.00-16.00

The former butter market in Helston has been turned into an intriguing museum. The building also serves as the Drill Hall and houses exhibits relating to the town and the Lizard peninsula. Of particular note are the displays about serpentine and the war. The display about Bob Fitzsimmons, a local pugilist, is another reason to visit. Don't forget the mezzanine gallery which is used for arts and crafts displays throughout the year.

MEVAGISSEY MUSEUM

Address: Mevagissey Museum, East Wharf, Inner Harbour, Mevagissey

Phone: 01726 843568

Website: www.mevagisseymuseum.co.uk

Opening times: From Easter to October; Daily from 11.00- 16.00. From July to August; Daily from 11.00 – 17.00

This delightful museum is a real piece of history as the building itself was used to build boats for smuggling in the eighteenth century. At one time this was a hive of activity with a carpenter on the first floor, storage at the top and boats being made in the ground floor and yard. Today there are exhibits relating to the fishing and boat building industry in Mevagissey and it is a lovely place to spend a while learning about the history of the area. Other items of interest include the exhibits of Pears Soap as Andrew Pears came from Mevagissey.

CORNISH STUDIES LIBRARY

Address: Cornish Studies Library, Alma Place, Redruth, TR15 2AT

Phone: 01209 216 760

Website: www.cornwall.gov.uk

Opening times: Mon, Tues, Thur, Fri 10.00-17.00, Sat 10.00-13.00, Wed Closed

The Cornish Studies Library in Redruth is a collection of books, newspapers and other resources on Cornwall. It is staffed by specialist librarians who are experts in helping those studying various aspects of Cornwall. It is a fascinating resource for those researching family history or another aspect of Cornwall.

LOSTWITHIEL MUSEUM

Address: 16, Fore Street, Lostwithiel, PL22 0BW

Phone: 01208 873005

Opening times: Easter to the end of September; Mon- Sat 10.30-16.30

The town of Lostwithiel was a major port in the 12th century and is steeped in history. This small museum is a treasure trove of facts about the town and local families. In summer there are also guided walks of Lostwithiel each Thursday from 11 am starting outside the museum, weather permitting. The museum and walks are staffed by volunteers.

ST AGNES MUSEUM

Address: Penwinnick Road, St Agnes, Cornwall, TR5 0PA

Phone: 01872 553228

Website: www.stagnesmuseum.org.uk

Opening times: Open daily from 10.30-17.00 April until October

St Agnes Museum is a fascinating collection of artefacts from the historic village and includes exhibits on the mining history as well as art from John Opie, a local artist. The turtle is particularly popular with young visitors and people come from all over the world to use the family history resources.

CALLINGTON HERITAGE CENTRE

Address: Liskeard Road, Callington

Phone: 01579 389506

Website: www.callingtonheritage.org.uk

Opening times: Easter to October; Fri, Sat, Sun 10.00-16.00

This delightful museum has a display of the Callington history as well as some from surrounding villages. From posters and photographs to chapel china and costumes this is an interesting collection and there are family history resources at the centre too.

LAWRENCE HOUSE, LAUNCESTON

Address: 9 Castle Street, Launceston, Cornwall, PL15 8BA

Phone: 01566 773277

Website: www.lawrencehousemuseum.org.uk

Opening times: Mon 2nd Apr- 2nd Nov; Mon-Fri 10.30-16.30 (last entry at 16.00)

This fine Georgian house in Launceston is steeped in history and has a fine collection of exhibits. These include the history of the Launceston area, a wonderful toy room, and a model railway. There is also a very interesting display about the life and work of Charles Causley, a poet who lived in the town, and lots more in the rooms of this beautiful house. Castle Street itself has been described by Sir John Betjeman as, "Having the most perfect collection of 18th century townhouses in Cornwall."

PENRYN MUSEUM

Address: Town Hall, Higher Market Street, Penryn, TR10 8LT

Phone: 01326 372158

Website:
http://www.museumsincornwall.org.uk/museums/penryn-museum

Opening times: Mon-Fri 10.00-15.30

Penryn Museum is a small collection of interesting pieces from the town and surrounding area.

DAVIDSTOW MOOR RAF MEMORIAL MUSEUM

Address: Davidstow, Camelford, PL32 9YF

Phone: 01840213266

Website: www.davidstowmemorialmuseum.co.uk

Opening times: Daily from 10.00- 16.00 from Easter to October.

In 1942 the small aerodrome on Davidstow Moor opened and was first used by Americans before they went to France. Today the museum has a very interesting display of the history of this airfield with many stories of bravery and the strategic importance of this small place.

GERRANS HERITAGE AND INFORMATION CENTRE

Address: The Old Forge, Tregassick Road, Gerrans

Phone: 01872 580535

Website: www.gerransheritage.co.uk

Opening times: Mon-Sat from April to October 14.00-16.00. Check website for the most up to date times.

This is a fascinating collection of items and genealogy from the Gerrans area. The small museum includes shipwright and farming tools, and memories from the Second World War.

CORNWALL FAMILY HISTORY SOCIETY

Address: 18, Lemon Street, Truro, TR1 2LS

Phone: 01872 264044

Website: www.cornwallfhs.com

Opening times: Mon, Wed, Thurs, Fri: 11.00-15.00, Sat: 10.00-13.00, Tues, Sun: Closed

This is a library full of interesting documents relating to Cornish family history and the county itself. It is an excellent resource for anyone tracing their family history and for finding out more about Cornwall and its past.

MARCONI CENTRE

Poldhu, Mullion. TR12 7JB

Phone: 01326 241656

Website: www.marconi-centre-poldhu.org.uk

Opening times: October to April; Sun 13.30-16.30, Tues and Fri 19.00-21.00. May, June, Sept; Sun and Wed 13.30-16.30, Tues and Fri 19.00-21.00. July and August; Sun, Wed, Thurs 13.30-16.00, Tues and Fri 19.00-21.00

The Marconi Centre was built in 2001 to celebrate the centenary of the first transatlantic signal. There is a film and display of Marconi's work and the connection with Poldhu in this very interesting museum.

SALTASH HERITAGE MUSEUM

Address: 17, Lower Fore St, Saltash, Cornwall PL12 6JQ

Phone: 01752 848466

Website: www.saltash-heritage.co.uk

Opening times: April to June; Wednesdays 2.00 pm - 4.00 pm , Saturdays 10.00 am - 4.00 pm. July to September; Wednesdays 2.00 pm - 4.00 pm , Fridays 10.30 am - 12.30 pm, Saturdays 10.00 am - 4.00 pm . October to November; Wednesdays 2.00 pm - 4.00 pm , Saturdays 10.00 am - 4.00 pm , Bank Holiday Mondays 10.00 am - 4.00 pm

This is a small but interesting collection of material relating to Saltash and the surrounding area. The museum also holds a themed exhibition on something of local interest each year.

MULLION HERITAGE CENTRE

Located in the chapel in Mullion

Opening times: Mon, Wed, Sat 14.00-16.00

The new museum in Mullion is a relatively new addition to the village and has interesting displays about the area including one about the history of the harbour.

BEAUTIFUL BEACHES

Cornwall is full of delightful coves, surfing beaches and stretches of sand that are wonderful for a winter walk or a summer day with a picnic, bucket and spade. A few suggestions are included and you may of course discover others for yourself.

CARBIS BAY, ST IVES

Carbis Bay has been the setting for Rosamunde Pilcher novels and is a beautiful beach just outside St Ives. Sheltered by tree covered cliffs this is a great place for bathing and can be reached by road, bus or train. There are toilets and a small café on the beach itself.

POLRIDMOUTH COVE

Many walkers on the Fowey to St Austell part of the South West Coastal Footpath discover Polridmouth en route. This is a sheltered cove which faces south and actually divides into two beaches at high tide. Access can be tricky and is down a long farm track so this beach may not be suitable for everyone and parking is available in Menabilly, three quarters of a mile away. There are no other facilities at this beach and it appeals to those who want to get away from the crowds.

KYNANCE COVE, LIZARD

With dramatic serpentine cliffs the beach at Kynance Cove is one of the most attractive in Cornwall. The rock formations are one of its defining features and it is a lovely place to spend a sunny day. The National Trust Car Park has a charge from Easter to November but there is free parking in The Lizard and a footpath leading to Kynance Cove. A café and toilets are available at Kynance Cove.

SUMMERLEAZE BEACH, BUDE

Cornwall has a number of beaches where there are sand chairs for hire and Summerleaze Beach at Bude is just one of them. The beach is accessed from the car park (charge applicable) which also has accessible loos, and is also within a short walk of the town centre. It is a large stretch of sand so hardly ever appears crowded and has a breakwater with tower as one of its more unusual features as well as surfing. There is also a safe bathing area at the sea water swimming pool area. Summerleaze has lifeguards from May to September.

HELFORD PASSAGE, NEAR FALMOUTH, CORNWALL

The swimming at Glebe Beach on the Helford Passage is a delight and there are a number of little coves all along this stretch of the water. Boat rides up the river for a charge are another great way to enjoy a sunny day. With an excellent pub or two in the area what more is needed for a peaceful day beside the sea.

HAYLE BEACH

With three miles of golden sands the beach at Hayle is among the best at any time of the year. There is surfing on this coast and visitors can either park in the car park or walk from town which takes around 20 minutes. The beach stretches from Hayle Towans to Black Cliff, Mexico Towans and across to Godrevy Point.

MAWGAN PORTH

For those that are unable to handle the crowds in Newquay Mawgan Porth is a quieter alternative. Just four miles from Newquay this is a lovely sandy beach with rock pools and ideal for families. The village also has some good places to eat and stay.

SENNEN

A long sandy beach in West Cornwall, Sennen is popular with surfers as well as families. The sea is very dramatic when the wind blows from the West, and Sennen's charming fishermen's cottages add to the beauty of this beach.

TOWAN BEACH, PORTH FARM, THE ROSELAND PENINSULA

This is a beautiful and quite remote beach on the way to St Anthony's Lighthouse. It is a sheltered spot so excellent for families who enjoy rock pools and paddling. The beach is accessed via some National Trust barns and a sea grass path towards the beach where the views are delightful.

POLKERRIS, NEAR FOWEY

Polkerris is a beautiful beach that is perfect for swimming and snorkelling. It is sheltered by a harbour wall at one end and also has an excellent beach café. Access is signposted off the A3082 St Austell to Fowey road.

WONDERFUL WILDLIFE

CORNISH CAMELS

Address: Rosuick Organic Farm, St Martin, Helston, TR12 6DZ

Phone: 01326 231 119

Website: www.cornishcamels.com

Opening times: May to September 10.30-17.00. October to April 11.00-16.00 Thurs, Fri, Sat

Located on an organic farm near Helston are a herd of ten camels which are quite a sight in the Cornish countryside. There is a farm trail to walk along and see the animals including cows and wallabies and also an excellent farm shop. Visiting this very interesting and unusual attraction is free.

BLUEBELL WOODS

Tehidy Country Park, near Camborne, Cornwall

Grid Reference: SW 65082 43279

Website: http://www.cornwall.gov.uk/default.aspx?page=13240

Tehidy Country Park is the largest woodland area in West Cornwall with around nine miles of open area to explore. This was once the country seat of the Bassett family and there are a number of walks on the old historic estate. In late May this becomes one of the best bluebell woods in Cornwall and is a stunning place to visit. Open all year round Tehidy has a visitor centre, toilets and is a great place to observe nature at any time of the year.

OBSERVE CORNISH CHOUGHS

Website: www.cornishchoughs.org

The Cornish Chough is the national bird of Cornwall and has recently been reintroduced into the county. Whilst no nature watching trip ever guarantees seeing specific birds or animals the best places to observe the elusive chough are on the walks from the Lizard to Kynance Cove and from Botallack Cliffs to Cape Cornwall. If you do happen to see a chough let the Cornwall Chough Project at www.cornishchoughs.org know and in particular the date, time, and place using a grid reference if possible. Record any distinguishing marks on the bird such as the rings and what colours they are. If you visit in April you can even take part in Chough Watch to record numbers of the birds along the coast and help the Cornwall Chough Project. It is worth looking at the Cornish Chough Project website before planning a visit as they offer free guided walks from time to time.

MOUSEHOLE BIRD HOSPITAL

Address: Raginnis Hill, Mousehole, Penzance, Cornwall, TR19 6SR

Website: www.mouseholebirdhospital.org.uk

Opening times: Open daily and visitors are welcome.

Mousehole Bird Hospital was founded in 1928 by Dorothy and Phyllis Yglesias. It grew in popularity over the years and shot to fame when hundreds of birds were treated following the Torrey Canyon disaster. Birds from all over Cornwall are cared for at this very special hospital before being released into the wild.

HAYLE ESTUARY

Located just west of Hayle Town

Grid reference: SW550370

Phone: 01736 711682

Located on the banks of the Hayle Estuary the Royal Society for the Protection of Birds (RSPB) has a hide and some parking for bird watchers. Expect to see a number of wading birds including migratory ducks, grebes, terns and many more.

MARAZION MARSH

Located to the west of Marazion town

Grid Reference: SW510312

Marazion Marsh is a Royal Society for the Protection of Birds (RSPB) Nature Reserve and has some lovely views of St Michael's Mount. This is an excellent place for bird watching and is particularly known for migratory species as well as aerial displays by starlings. It is also somewhere to see dragonflies and wild flowers.

GREAT WALKS

Walking is one of the best ways to see the Cornish countryside. A few are listed but there are many more and lots of good walking guides. Don't forget to take a map and wear the correct gear when walking and to take care on paths, particularly on the cliffs.

GREAT FLAT LODE

OS MAP: 104 **Grid reference:** SW 678396

The Great Flat Lode takes its name from a huge body of ore tilted at 45 degrees just south of Carn Brea. The walking trail named after it encompasses all the disused mines in the Camborne and Redruth area and around Carn Brea. This is a great cycling route as well as a walking trail and is around 7.5 miles in length. Visitors walking the trail can see some of the old buildings, particularly at South Wheal Frances (Grid Ref: SW678393). The engine houses at East Pool and Agar (Grid ref: SW674415) are also a highlight of the circular walk.

ROCKY VALLEY, BOSSINEY, TINTAGEL, PL34 0BB

OS MAP: Landrager 200 **Grid Ref:** SX 073891

This is a short walk of around 1.5 miles with an incredible amount to see in such a short distance. Park your car in the layby near Rocky Valley, and cross the road towards Trevillet Mill continuing down the drive. Then cross the footbridge and continue through the woods towards the Trewethett Mill, once used for yarn making. Bronze Age carvings on a rock face can be seen along this trail. Close by is St Nectan's Glen with a waterfall flowing into the stream. This is where King Arthur's Knights are said to have been baptised before heading off in search of the Holy Grail. By crossing another footbridge and following the stream downwards you will come to the cliff top for some spectacular coastal views. This is an area where Thomas Hardy wrote many of his "Emma" poems and where there are lots of wild flowers including bluebells in season. Return using the same path that you came down.

BOTALLACK TO ZENNOR

OS MAP: 102 **Grid Ref:** SW362336

This is one of the most spectacular walks in Cornwall and takes in the South West Coastal Footpath. It is around 10 miles long and takes in the dramatic scenery around Cape Cornwall, Crown Mines perched on the Botallack Cliffs, and Pendeen with Levant Mine. The Bosigran Cliffs are also on the walk as is Gurnards Head and finally the village of Zennor. The walk can be done in either direction and there is also a circular route back via St Just.

ST AGNES BEACON

OS MAP: 104   **Grid Ref:** SW 698515

St Agnes Beacon has panoramic views across Cornwall and on a clear day St Ives can be seen from the summit as well as China Clay country and Trevose Head near Padstow. From the St Agnes Village car Park the walk passes Higher Bal to the summit and takes around an hour. In previous years a fire would be lit from the summit to warn of danger such as invasion and these days is used as more of a celebration. There are choices of paths from the Beacon back down to St Agnes and one option is to take the main path via Goonvrea to the village or a more challenging route along St Agnes Head and the coast.

KIT HILL COUNTRY PARK

Kit Hill, Callington, Cornwall, PL17 8HW

Phone: 01579 370030

Website: www.cornwall.gov.uk

This is a magnificent granite hill with splendid views and set amongst 400 acres of country park in the Tamar Valley. There is a network of paths with great trails and views across Dartmoor and Bodmin Moor. Kit Hill also has the remains of a 19th century mine and an ancient Neolithic long barrow amongst its archaeological sites.

CALLINGTON MURAL TRAIL

Callington, Cornwall

Website: www.callington-tc.gov.uk

For an unusual but vibrant walk take a stroll around Callington which is famous for its tow murals. These have been painted by locals and professionals on various walls in the area and form a walk with a difference. Pick up a trail leaflet from the tourist office in town and begin your artistic stroll around Callington. Some celebrate the Callington Honey Fair, others show people and some have a wonderful 3D effect.

CADGWITH TO POLTESCO

Grid Ref: SW7214

This is a 2 mile circular walk which starts in Cadgwith and heads towards beautiful Carleon Cove and via a ruined serpentine factory through Ruan Minor and the road back to Cadgwith.

WALK ALONG CARN BREA

Redruth

Grid Ref: SW 68644086

Carn Brea dominates the Redruth skyline and from the summit there are wonderful views across the county. There is a monument to the Basset family, a hunting lodge and some trails for walking. Iron Age hut settlements can also be found across the summit. It is possible to drive up a track from the Eastern end of Carn Brea but the trails are for people with stout footwear.

FABULOUS FESTIVALS

Cornwall has a host of unique and spectacular festivals which are free to visit and create their own special atmosphere. Here are just a few to consider as part of your holiday plans.

HELSTON FLORA DAY

Website: www.helstonfloraday.org.uk

Held on the 8th May each year (unless 8th May is on a Sunday in which case it occurs on the preceding Saturday) and is an ancient festival held in the town of Helston. The people of the town dance through the streets and even in and out of some of the houses en route. Leaders of the dance must have been born in Helston and can only lead once in their lifetime. The best dances to watch are the midday dance when the townsfolk are dressed in beautiful costumes and also the children's dance at 10.00. The Helston Town Band leads the dancers through a traditional route playing the famous tune and there are lots of other celebrations on the day including an ancient Celtic Rite called Hal and Tow. This is a way of welcoming springtime and new life, and is worth a journey to the area to join in the fun.

MURDOCH DAY

Redruth Town Centre, Redruth

Each June the town of Redruth celebrates one of their most famous inhabitants, William Murdoch, who invented gas lighting. For one day only the town comes alive in a pageant of parades, art activities and celebrations. Murdoch was born in Scotland in 1754 and moved to Redruth in 1779 where the first house to be lit by gas still stands. In Redruth Murdoch Day is a celebratory occasion and fun to come along and see.

GOLOWAN

Website: www.golowan.org

Golowan is "The Feast of St John the Baptist", in Cornish and is celebrated in Penzance with an arts festival and carnival atmosphere. There are stalls in the streets, music and other processions. This is a Midsummer festival held in June and is worth a visit to Penzance to see their version of the Obby Oss and other traditional fun in the streets. Whilst the street entertainment is free there are charges for some of the concerts held during the event.

FOWEY REGATTA

Website: http://www.foweyroyalregatta.co.uk

Fowey Regatta is held during August and is considered one of the best in the country. Events around Town Quay and the gig racing are just some of the festivities to be enjoyed by visitors and locals alike. Even the Red Arrows put in an appearance at one of the best sailing events in the west.

LAFROWDA

Website: www.lafrowda-festival.co.uk

Lafrowda is a community celebration of the arts which takes place in St Just in Penwith each year during July. There are arts related events all over town culminating in a live music celebration in town on the peak day in July. The Lafrowda website is the best way to check out dates and events of this vibrant festival.

PADSTOW OBBY OSS DAY

Website: http://www.padstow.com/obby_oss/obby_oss.php

One of the best known celebrations in Cornwall, the first of May is Obby Oss Day in Padstow and well worth a day out. The Red Oss or original one and the Blue Peace Oss weave their way through the town and people born in Padstow wear the colours showing their allegiance to the particular Oss. The dance and song are unique to the town with celebrations going on all day. Obby Oss Day is thought to be a celebration of the arrival of spring and an ancient fertility rite.

CORNISH PASTY FESTIVAL

Website: www.redruth-tc.gov.uk

In September the mining heritage of Cornwall is celebrated with a three day festival. This focuses on Miner's Day and the cultural heritage remembered at St Euny Church, and a pasty festival which celebrates Cornwall's famous food. There is music, a market and all manner of festivities in the town over this weekend in September.

WATCH HURLING AT ST IVES

Hurling is part of the traditions of St Ives. As part of the celebrations for St Ives Feast there is a traditional game of hurling in town on Feast Monday (the Sunday nearest the 3rd February is the saint's day itself.) At 10.30 the Mayor of St Ives starts the game by hurling a sliver ball into the crowd. It is passed from one another on the beach and then into the streets of St Ives. Whoever has the ball when the town clock strikes noon takes it to the mayor for a reward.

WRITERS AND FILMS IN CORNWALL

BETJEMAN'S CHURCHES

John Betjeman loved Cornwall and two churches in particular are associated with him. "Blessed be St Enodoc, " refers to one of his favourite churches and where he is buried in the churchyard. St Enodoc Church is in the midst of the golf course of the same name and above the cliffs of Daymer Bay. This makes a pleasant walk out to see the church which is half buried in the sand and which meant so much to Sir John Betjeman. At the Church of St Endellion the approach has been described as, "like a ring of bells," and was another of Sir John Betjeman's favourites.

DOC MARTIN'S FILM LOCATIONS

Doc Martin is a popular TV show and most of the outside scenes are shot in Port Isaac. Fern Cottage in the village is the Doc's house. Other outside scenes were filmed in Port Gaverne where the Headland Hotel is actually Mrs Wilson's hotel. The non-wedding between Doc Martin and Louisa was filmed at Lanteglos Church near Camelford. The Old Inn at St Breward is where the birth of the baby was filmed, and there are many other places in North Cornwall associated with the Doc Martin series.

LEGENDARY PLACES

There are legends all over the Cornish countryside including tales of giants, mermaids and even Arthurian tales. Many of the places associated with them can be visited free of charge.

ZENNOR CHURCH

The Mermaid of Zennor is one of Cornwall's most famous legends. In the village of Zennor the Church of St Senara has a pew end where visitors can see a mermaid carved into the wood. The legend centres around a local boy named Matthew Trewella, who always sang the evening song in this church. One day a mermaid from nearby Pendour Cove heard the singing and disguising herself with a cloak, walked up to the church to listen. She repeated this every day but knew she would have to return to the sea or die. One day she told Matthew who by this time had fallen in love with her. He carried her down to the sea and they both disappeared into the waves and were never seen again. It is said that on some days you can hear the voice of Matthew Trewella singing in Pendour Cove.

MERLIN'S CAVE, TINTAGEL

Legend has it that Merlin lived below King Arthur's Castle in a cave. Below the ruined fortress at Tintagel two caves can be reached via a steep cliff path at low tide only and are thought to be the ones from the legendary tale. This is not suitable for some visitors due to the steepness and any visitor should take note of the tides and weather if deciding to visit this cave.

DOZMARY POOL

Grid Ref: SX 195745

Located on Bodmin Moor, Dozmary Pool is reputed to be
bottomless and is where Sir Bedivere is said to have thrown
Excalibur. King Arthur received his mortal would at the Battle
of Camlan and a possible site is at Slaughter Bridge on the
River Cam which is just ten miles from Dozmary Pool.
Summer droughts and a car accident have proved Dozmary
Pool to have a bottom but its links with Arthurian legend are
worth exploring. As no stream drains into it the pool remains
an enigma as to its existence to this day.

A TASTE OF CORNWALL

Cornwall is renowned for its fine food and there are a number of places where visitors can see the product being made and perhaps get a chance to taste it.

CORNISH ORCHARDS CIDER

Address: Westnorth Manor Farm, Duloe, Liskeard, Cornwall, PL14 4PW

Phone: 01503 263373

Website: www.cornishorchards.co.uk

Opening times: Easter to October; Mon-Fri: 10.00- 17.00, Sat 9.30-12.00. Nov- April; Wed: 10.00- 17.00, Sat: 10.00- 12.30

Just outside Liskeard the cider production at Cornish Orchards relies on locally sourced apples. Many varieties grown here are of the old Cornish variety such as Rattler and Lord of the Isles. If the staff have time they show visitors around although guided tours are not routinely offered. Tasting apple juice and cider from the shop is another highlight of a visit to Cornish Orchards.

TRENANCE CHOCOLATES

Address: Mullion Meadows, Mullion, Helston, Cornwall, TR12 7HB

Phone: 01326 241499

Website: www.trenancechocolate.co.uk

Opening times: Open 7 days a week but phone ahead to check timings as there are seasonal working hours.

Trenance Chocolates is located near Helston and uses the finest ingredients. Luxury chocolates are crafted before visitor's eyes and there may also be a bit of tasting as well. Just try coming out of the shop empty handed.

HEALEY'S CORNISH CYDER FARM

Address: Penhallow, Truro, Cornwall, TR4 9LW

Phone: 01872 573356

Website: www.thecornishcyderfarm.co.uk

Opening times: all year round with a break over the Christmas and New Year period. The website has a helpful chart for more up to date opening times as these do vary through the year.

Healey's is a working cider farm just outside Truro where visitors can see the wine, scrumpy and brandy being made. There are friendly farm animals here for children and a shop and restaurant. This is a free venue but there is a charge for the guided tours.

GLORIOUS GARDENS

QUEEN MARY GARDENS, FALMOUTH

Address: Queen Mary Gardens, Gyllyngvase Beach, Falmouth

Phone: 01326312300

Opening times: open all year

Not far from popular Gyllyngvase Beach the Queen Mary Gardens have a beautiful display of sub-tropical flowers, many of which are not seen in other parts of the UK. The layout is accessible to wheelchair users and there is also a café here. There are some really colourful displays of flowers throughout spring and summer.

HEARTLANDS DIASPORA GARDENS

Address: Heartlands, Robinson's Shaft, Dudnance Lane, Pool, Cornwall, TR15 3QY

Phone: 01209 722322

Website: www.heartlandscornwall.com

There is a traditional Cornish saying that wherever there is a mine you will find a Cornishman. When miners left Cornwall to find work abroad they went to Australia, Mexico and South Africa to name just a few countries. The Diaspora Gardens in the Heartlands Project feature plants that grew in the places that the Cornish miners travelled to and are very interesting to visit to learn more of this part of local history.

VICTORIA GARDENS

Truro, Cornwall, TR1 1EA

Phone: 01872 274555

Located beside the River Kenwyn in Truro the Victoria Gardens are filled with exotic shrubs and colourful flowers. In summer there is usually a concert from the bandstand on a Sunday afternoon. This is a great place for a picnic on a summer day.

TREGENNA CASTLE GARDENS, ST IVES

Address: Tregenna Castle Hotel, St Ives, Cornwall

Website: www.tregenna-castle.co.uk

For a glorious view across St Ives Bay and a feast of sub-tropical flowers the gardens at Tregenna Castle are worth a look. It is the perfect place to escape the crowded streets in St Ives and to enjoy a sunset over the sea. The nature trail through the 72 acres of grounds is another wonderful way of spending an afternoon in St Ives.

KIMBERLY PARK GARDENS, FALMOUTH

This is a seven acre site just a fifteen minute walk from the sea and planted with some beautiful ornamental trees and plants. It is a wonderful place to relax on a hot day and for a break from the beaches.

GYLLYNGDUNE GARDENS, FALMOUTH

These splendid gardens were completed in 1907 and have a bandstand and the Princess Pavilion. A walk through these gardens could pass the rose garden, the secret grotto and out on to the seafront where there are some lovely views. Look out for band concerts in the gardens from time to time.

FOX ROSEHILL GARDENS, FALMOUTH

Melvill Road, Falmouth

Just off Melvill Road is one of Falmouth's best kept free secrets. Fox Rosehill Gardens is a wonderful collection of subtropical plants, many of which originated from seeds brought back by sea captains. The gardens were given to Falmouth at the end of World War Two by the Fox Rosehill family and are just a five minute walk from the town or seafront.

CARREG DHU COMMUNITY GARDENS

Address: Carreg Dhu, Longstone Road, Hugh Town, St Marys, Isles of Scilly

Carreg Dhu means "Black Rocks" and is a beautiful community garden with sub- tropical plants. It is manned by volunteers and has many quiet places to sit.

THE SPIRIT OF CORNWALL

PADSTOW LIFEBOAT STATION

Directions: Five miles out of Padstow on Trevose Head. Parking is via a toll road on the headland.

Phone: 01841 520861

Website: www.padstow-lifeboat.org.uk

Opening times: Mon-Fri 10.00-16.00

The lifeboat station at Padstow is open to the public and is a great opportunity to see the boat and learn about the work of the crew.

FISHERMAN'S FRIENDS

Port Isaac, Cornwall

Website: http://portisaacsfishermansfriends.com/

The Fisherman's Friends are a group of local men who sing in the Platt in Port Isaac on most Friday evenings. One day they were spotted by a recording studio and the rest is history. They are now a victim of their own success with crowds coming to Port Isaac for the free Friday concerts and have had to limit performances, particularly at high tide. The website gives a list of when the group are singing on the Platt in Port Isaac.

HELICOPTER SPOTTING

The Royal Naval Air Station (RNAS) Culdrose is one of the largest in Europe and is constantly busy patrolling and rescuing from the seas off Cornwall and the Western Approaches. Just outside Helston on the road towards The Lizard Culdrose has a public viewing enclosure where helicopters can be seen landing and taking off. Guided tours can be reserved and are at additional charge.

ATTEND A SERVICE AT GWENNAP PIT

Gwennap Pit, Busveal, St Day, TR16 5HH

Phone: 01209 822770

Website: www.gwennappit.co.uk

Gwennap Pit is an open air amphitheatre near Redruth and was made famous by John Wesley. This was a favourite place for John Wesley to preach and he did so 18 times between 1762 and 1789. Since 1807 there has been an open air service at Whitsun and the website is the best place to check for forthcoming services at this famous amphitheatre. When services are not being held Gwennap Pit is also open to the public to view the hollow.

VISIT FALMOUTH LIFEBOAT STATION

Address: Tinners Walk, Falmouth, TR11 3XZ

Phone: 01326 318375

Website: www.falmouthlifeboat.co.uk

Falmouth Lifeboat Station offer guided tours of the boat and equipment which is very popular. On occasions they restrict visitor numbers and are also required in emergencies. It is essential to contact the station beforehand to verify timing and whether the public are able to visit on a particular day as this is variable.

5053991R00032

Printed in Great Britain
by Amazon.co.uk, Ltd.,
Marston Gate.